Sister of Mine

A Heartwarming
Collection of
Letters, Writings
and Poetry

ISBN 1-889116-08-4

Printed in the United States of America

First U.S. Edition

Design by
Paragon Communications Group, Inc., Tulsa, Oklahoma

Pubiished by

PENBROOKE PUBLISHING

Tulsa, Oklahoma

ACKNOWLEDGEMENTS

Alcott, Louisa May: "To Anna" taken from *Louisa May Alcott, Life, Letters and Journals*, edited by Ednah D. Cheney. Random House Value Publishing, 1995. **Garner, Helen:** Excerpt from "A Scrapbook, An Album," by Helen Garner taken from *Sisters: Six Australian Writers Explore the Joys and the Frustrations of Being a Sister*, edited by Drusilla Modjeska. Angus & Robertson Publications, an imprint of HarperCollins Australia. **Grealy, Lucy:** Fragment from "The Other Half" taken from *Sister to Sister* by Patricia Foster. Copyright © 1995 by Patricia Foster. Used by permission of Doubleday, a division of Bantam Doubleday Dell Publishing Group, Inc. **Mansfield, Katherine:** Excerpt from "The Doll's House" taken from *The Short Stories of Katherine Mansfield*. Copyright © 1923 by Alfred A. Knopf, Inc. **Mead, Margaret:** Excerpts taken from *Blackberry Winter: My Earlier Years*, by Margaret Mead. William Morrow and Company, 1972. **Pogrebin, Letty Cottin:** Fragment from "Sisters and Secrets" taken from *Sister to Sister* by Patricia Foster. Copyright © 1995 by Patricia Foster. Used by permission of Doubleday, a division of Bantam Doubleday Dell Publishing Group, Inc.

Sister of Mine

A Heartwarming Collection of Letters, Writings and Poetry

PENBROOKE
PUBLISHING

Tulsa, Oklahoma

Dedicated To:

Kelly Dorsey Traldi

My sister; my friend

With much love always,

♡ Lori ♡

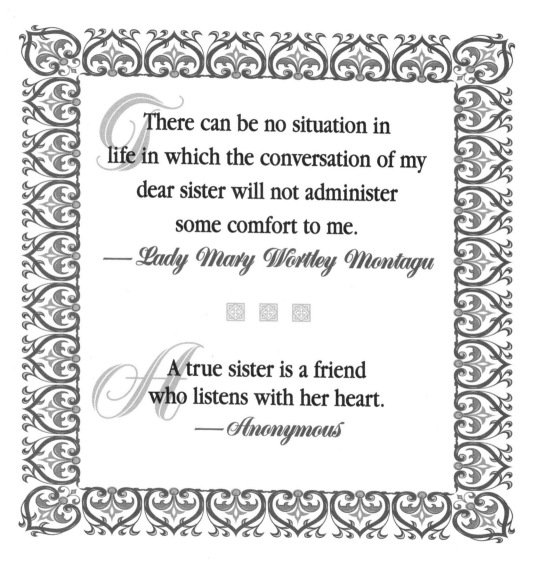

There can be no situation in
life in which the conversation of my
dear sister will not administer
some comfort to me.
— *Lady Mary Wortley Montagu*

A true sister is a friend
who listens with her heart.
— *Anonymous*

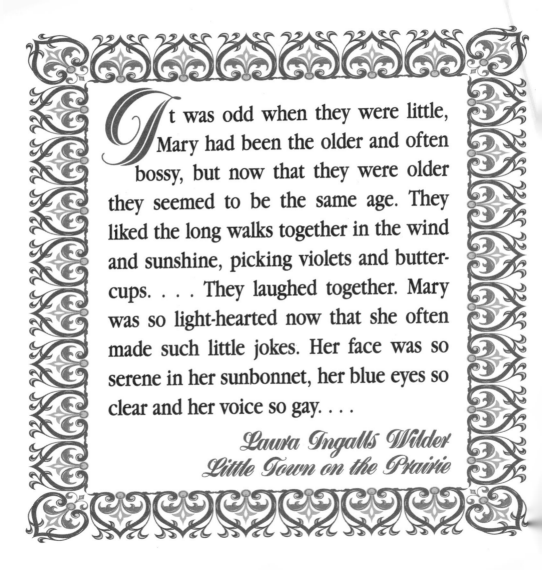

*I*t was odd when they were little, Mary had been the older and often bossy, but now that they were older they seemed to be the same age. They liked the long walks together in the wind and sunshine, picking violets and butter-cups. . . . They laughed together. Mary was so light-hearted now that she often made such little jokes. Her face was so serene in her sunbonnet, her blue eyes so clear and her voice so gay. . . .

Laura Ingalls Wilder
Little Town on the Prairie

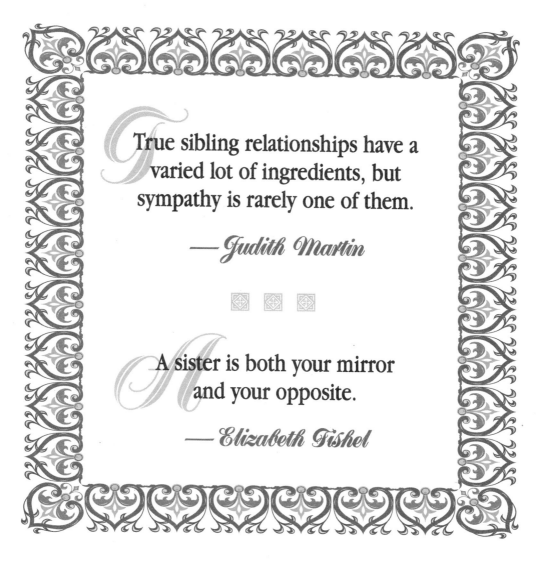

True sibling relationships have a varied lot of ingredients, but sympathy is rarely one of them.

— *Judith Martin*

A sister is both your mirror and your opposite.

— *Elizabeth Fishel*

To Anna

Sister, dear, when you are lonely,
Longing for your distant home,
And the images of loved ones
Warmly to your heart shall come,
Then, mid tender thoughts and fancies,
Let one fond voice say to thee,
"Ever when your heart is heavy,
Anna, dear, then think of me."

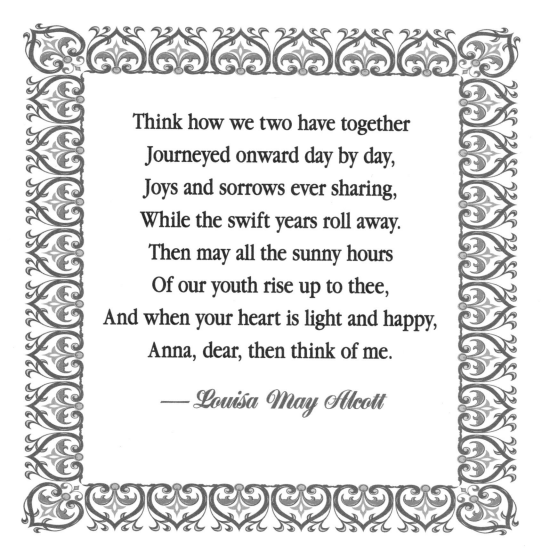

Think how we two have together
Journeyed onward day by day,
Joys and sorrows ever sharing,
While the swift years roll away.
Then may all the sunny hours
Of our youth rise up to thee,
And when your heart is light and happy,
Anna, dear, then think of me.

— *Louisa May Alcott*

A perfect sister I am not,
But I'm thankful for the one I've got.

— *Anonymous*

A family faces are magic mirrors.
Looking at people who belong to us,
we see the past, present, and future.

— *Gail Lumet Buckley*

There Was a Little Girl

There was a little girl
Who had a little curl
Right in the middle of her forehead.
When she was good
She was very, very good,
But when she was bad she was horrid.

— *Henry Wadsworth Longfellow*

I cannot deny that, now I am without your company I feel not only that I am deprived of a very dear sister, but that I have lost half of myself.

— *Beatrice d'Este, writing to her sister Isabella*

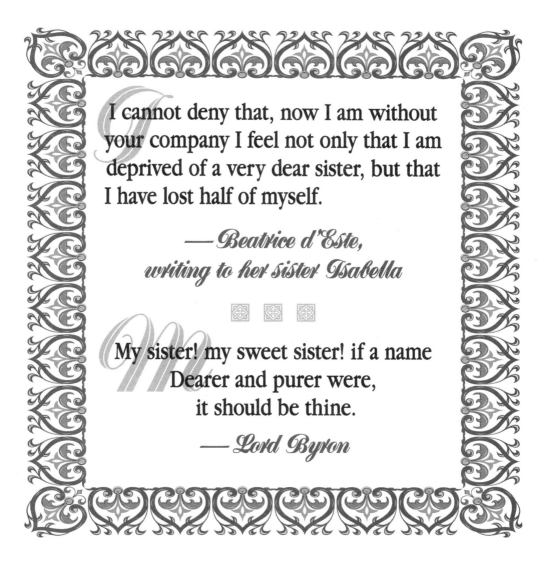

My sister! my sweet sister! if a name
Dearer and purer were,
it should be thine.

— *Lord Byron*

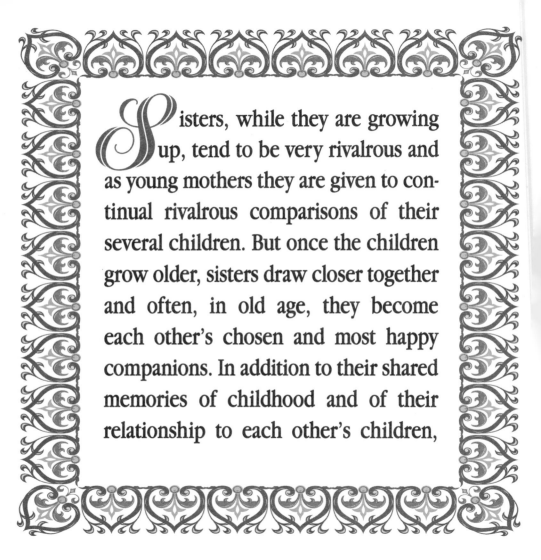

Sisters, while they are growing up, tend to be very rivalrous and as young mothers they are given to continual rivalrous comparisons of their several children. But once the children grow older, sisters draw closer together and often, in old age, they become each other's chosen and most happy companions. In addition to their shared memories of childhood and of their relationship to each other's children, they share memories of the same home, the same homemaking style, and the same small prejudices about housekeeping that carry the echoes of their mother's voice. . . . But above all, perhaps, sisters who have grown up close to one another know how their daydreams have been interwoven with their life experiences.

— *Margaret Mead*
Blackberry Winter

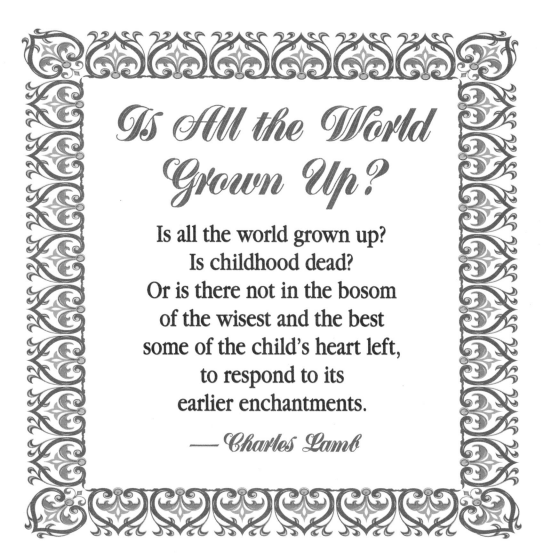

Is All the World Grown Up?

Is all the world grown up?
Is childhood dead?
Or is there not in the bosom
of the wisest and the best
some of the child's heart left,
to respond to its
earlier enchantments.

— Charles Lamb

No Friend Like a Sister

For there is no friend like a sister
In calm and stormy weather;
To cheer one if one goes astray,
To lift one if one totters down,
To strengthen whilst one stands.

— *Christina Rossetti*
Goblin Market

My sister Jewelle was four years older that I. . . She was chatty and inquisitive, and related easily to grown-ups. She carried the confidence and assurance of the firstborn lightly on her shoulders.

— *Shirlee Taylor Haizlip*

We do not remember days,
we remember moments.

— *Cesare Pavese*

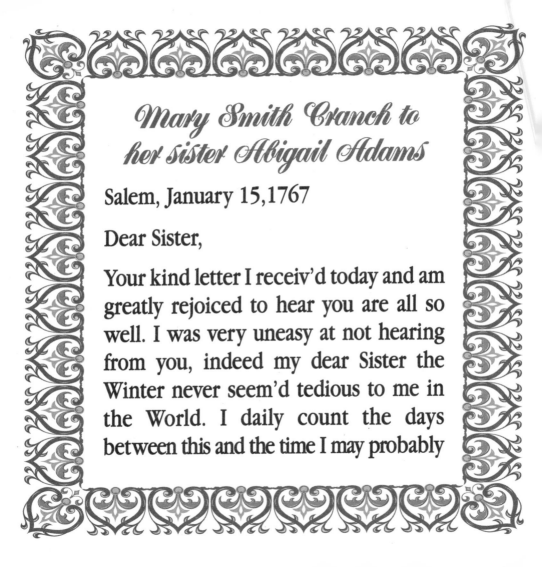

Mary Smith Cranch to her sister Abigail Adams

Salem, January 15, 1767

Dear Sister,

Your kind letter I receiv'd today and am greatly rejoiced to hear you are all so well. I was very uneasy at not hearing from you, indeed my dear Sister the Winter never seem'd tedious to me in the World. I daily count the days between this and the time I may probably see you. I could never feel so comfort-able as I at present do, if I thought I should spend another Winter here. Indeed my Sister I cannot bear the thought of staying here so far from all my Friends if Mr. Cranch can do as well nigher. I would give a great deal only to know I was within Ten Miles of you if I could not see you. Our children will never seem so natural to each other as if they liv'd where they could see one another oftener. . . .

Sisters are probably the most
competitive relationship
within the family,
but once the sisters are grown,
it becomes the strongest relationship.

— *Margaret Mead*

Big sisters are the crabgrass
in the lawn of life.

— *Charles M. Schulz*

She had come to be a friend and companion such as few possessed—intelligent, well-informed, useful, gentle, knowing all the ways of the family, interested in all its concerns, and peculiarly interested in Emma, in every pleasure, every scheme of hers; one to whom Emma could speak every thought as it arose, and who had such an affection for her as could never find fault.

—*Jane Austen*
Emma

A ministering angel shall my sister be.

— *William Shakespeare*

Never praise a sister to a sister,
in the hope of your compliment
ever reaching the proper ear.

— *Rudyard Kipling*

My dearest Arabel is, of course, here once if not twice a day, and for hours at a time, bringing me great joy always, and Henrietta's dear kindness in coming to London on purpose to see me, for a week, has left a perfume in my life. Both those beloved sisters have been, as ever, perfect to me.

— *Elizabeth Barrett Browning,*
writing about her sisters

According to popular myth, sisters exist on the same side of the closed door, sharing teddy bears and secrets in the privacy of a common bedroom.

— *Marianne Paul*

We must strengthen, defend, preserve and comfort each other.
We must love one another.

— *John Winthrop*

There is no time like the old time,
when you and I were young!

— *Oliver Wendell Holmes*

God gave us memories
that we might have roses
in December.

— *James M. Barrie*

Harriet Beecher Stowe to Sarah Beecher

December 1850

My dear Sister,

Is it really true that snow is on the ground and Christmas coming, and I have not written unto thee, most dear sister? No, I don't believe it! I haven't been so naughty–it's all a mistake–yes, written I must have–and written I have too–in the night watches as I lay on my bed–such beautiful letters–I wish you had only received them!

As for Louisa, I really think that in my life I never knew or heard of anything equal to the sweetness and gentleness of her disposition. She is indeed as yet quite an angel. She is mildness itself. It is not in nature to ruffle the sweetness of her temper one single instant.

— *Emily Lennox*

How vast a memory has Love!

— *Alexander Pope*

*B*etty is fourteen years older than I. She's the sister who lived at home until the morning of her wedding. She left when she was twenty-one and I was seven. She's the sister who taught me how to tell time, the sister who set her hair in bobby pins and combed it in a page-boy, the sister who dated handsome boys in uniform and wore leg make-up during World War II when stockings were rationed, the person I've always called my sister, and thought of as my sister, my real sister, my only sister, even though I discovered when I was twelve that she was born of a different father and was in fact my half sister. . . .

— *Letty Cottin Pogrebin*
"Sisters and Secrets"
Sister to Sister

We wove a web of childhood
A web of sunny air.

— *Charlotte Brontë*

We acquire friends and
we make enemies,
but our sisters come with
the territory.

— *Evelyn Loeb*

In Go-Cart So Tiny

In go-cart so tiny
My sister I drew;
And I've promised to draw her
The wide world through.
We have not yet started–
I own it with sorrow–
Because our trip's always
Put off till tomorrow.

— Kate Greenaway

My Sister

My sister!
With that thrilling word
Let thoughts unnumbered wildly spring!
What echoes in my heart are stirred,
While thus I touch the trembling string.

— Margaret Davidson

It is true that I was born in Iowa,
but I can't speak for my twin sister.

— Abigail Van Buren

It was rather a pretty little picture, for the sisters sat together in the shady nook, with sun and shadow flickering over them, the aromatic wind lifting their hair and cooling their hot cheeks, and all the little wood people going on with their affairs as if these were no strangers but old friends. Meg sat upon her cushion, sewing daintily with her white hands, and looking as fresh and sweet as a rose, in her pink dress, among the green. Beth was sorting the cones that lay thick under the hemlock near by, for she made pretty things of them. Amy was sketching a group of ferns, and Jo was knitting as she read aloud.

Louisa May Alcott
Little Women

Sisters are our peers,
the voices of our times.

— *Elizabeth Fishel*

An older sister helps one
remain half child, half woman.

— *Anonymous*

Whenever I try to live in another town, my phone bill rockets; and when I look carefully at the breakdown of the call times, I see that I make the largest number to my sisters between the hours of four and five p.m.— that is, after-school time. I am fifty but I still have this habit, this longing to hear their stories of the day. I want them to make me laugh.

— *Helen Garner*
"A Scrapbook, An Album"
Sisters

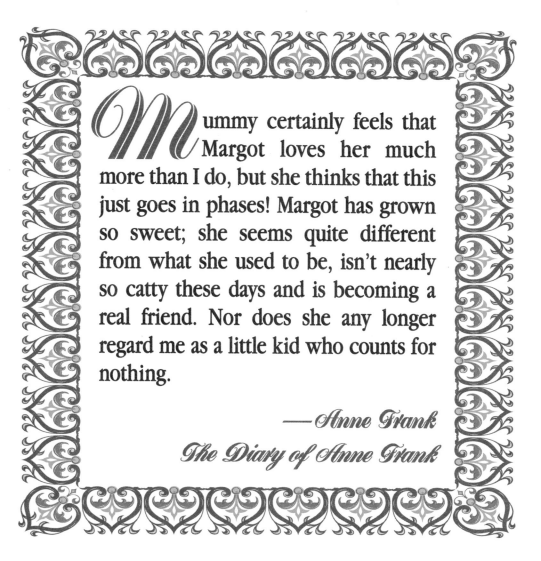

Mummy certainly feels that Margot loves her much more than I do, but she thinks that this just goes in phases! Margot has grown so sweet; she seems quite different from what she used to be, isn't nearly so catty these days and is becoming a real friend. Nor does she any longer regard me as a little kid who counts for nothing.

—Anne Frank
The Diary of Anne Frank

The Sisters

In the vine-shadows on the veranda,
under the yellow leaves,
in the cooling sun,
sit the two sisters.
Their slow voices run
like little winter creeks dwindled
by frost and wind,
and the square of sunlight
moves on the veranda.

They remember the gay young men
on their tall horses
who came courting; the dancing and
the smells of leather
and wine, the girls whispering
by the fire together:
even their dolls and ponies, all they
have left behind
moves in the yellow shadows on the
veranda.

— *Judith Wright*

But were another childhood-world
my share,
I would be born a little sister.

— *George Eliot*

Sisters may share the same mother
and father but appear
to come from different families.

— *Anonymous*

Skating

Laura's heart swelled. She felt herself a part of the wide land, of the far deep sky and the brilliant moonlight. She wanted to fly. But Carrie was little and almost afraid, so she took hold of Carrie's hand and said, "Let's slide. Come on, run!" With hands clasped, they ran a little way. Then with right foot first they slid on the smooth ice much farther than they had run. "On the moonpath, Carrie! Let's follow the moonpath," Laura cried. And so they ran and slid, and ran and slid again, on the glittering moonpath into the light from the silver moon. Farther and farther from shore they went, straight toward the high bank on the other side. They swooped and almost seemed to fly. If Carrie lost her balance, Laura held her up. If Laura was unsteady, Carrie's hand steadied her.

— *Laura Ingalls Wilder*
By the Shores of Silver Lake

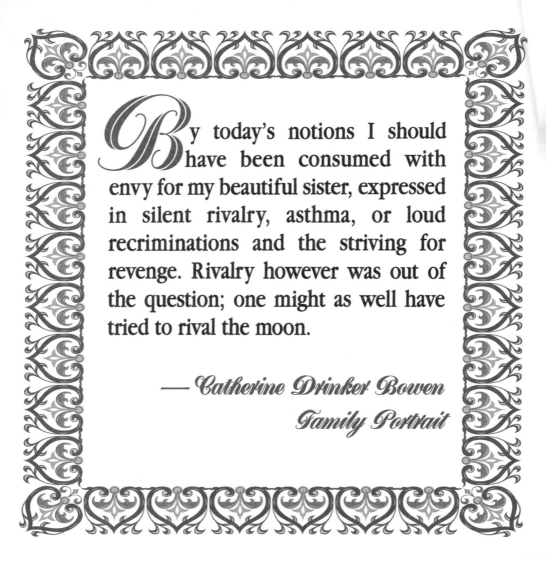

By today's notions I should have been consumed with envy for my beautiful sister, expressed in silent rivalry, asthma, or loud recriminations and the striving for revenge. Rivalry however was out of the question; one might as well have tried to rival the moon.

— *Catherine Drinker Bowen*
Family Portrait

The love that grew with us from our cradles never knew diminution from time or distance. Other ties were formed, but they did not supersede or weaken this. Death tore away all that was mortal and perishable, but this tie he could not sunder.

— *Charlotte Elizabeth Tonna*

Sisters stand between one and life's cruel circumstances.

— *Nancy Mitford*

How dear to this heart are the scenes
of my childhood,
When fond recollection presents
them to view!

— *Samuel Woodworth*

In thee my soul shall own combined
the sister and the friend.

— *Catharine Killigrew*

Louisa May Alcott to her sister Anne

(A thank-you for a surprise birthday party.)

My Own Dear Nan.

How shall I thank you for all the steps your dear feet have taken, all the hours spent in planning, all the love that kept your tender heart at work for me? I can't, & I won't try now, but it has touched me very much to find myself so loved, so anxiously cared for & remembered.

For when three sisters love each other with such sincere affection, the one does not experience sorrow, pain, or affliction of any kind, but the others' heart wishes to relieve, and vibrates in tenderness. Like a well-organized musical instrument.

— *Elizabeth Shaw, writing about her sisters Abigail Adams and Mary Cranch*

Margaret, the eldest of the four, was sixteen, and very pretty, being plump and fair, with large eyes, plenty of soft, brown hair, a sweet mouth, and white hands, of which she was rather vain. Fifteen-year-old Jo was very tall, thin and brown, and reminded one of a colt; for she never seemed to know what to do with her long limbs, which were very much in her way. She had a decided mouth, a comical nose, and sharp, grey eyes, which appeared to see everything, and were by turns fierce, funny or thoughtful. . . . Elizabeth, or

Beth, as everyone called her, was a rosy, smooth-haired, bright-eyed girl of thirteen, with a shy manner, a timid voice, and a peaceful expression, which was seldom disturbed. . . . Amy, though the youngest, was a most important person, in her own opinion at least. A regular snow-maiden, with blue eyes, and yellow hair, curling on her shoulders, pale and slender, and always carrying herself like a young lady.

— *Louisa May Alcott*
Little Women

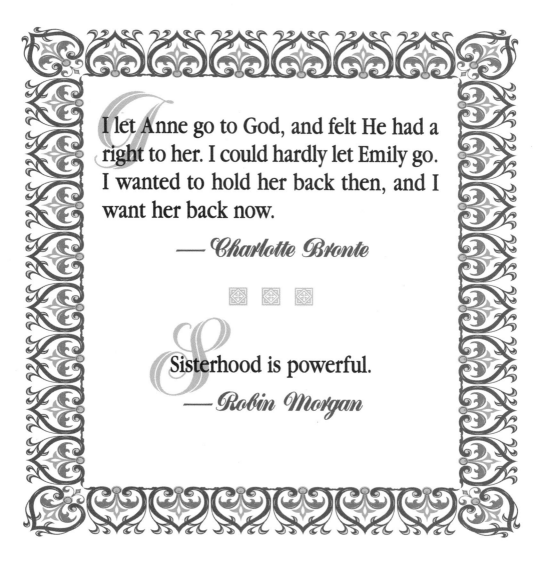

I let Anne go to God, and felt He had a right to her. I could hardly let Emily go. I wanted to hold her back then, and I want her back now.

— *Charlotte Bronte*

Sisterhood is powerful.

— *Robin Morgan*

Where Lil went our Elsie followed. In the playground, on the road going to and from school, there was Lil marching in front and our Elsie holding on behind. Only when she wanted anything, or when she was out of breath, our Elsie gave Lil a tug, a twitch, and Lil stopped and turned round. The Kelveys never failed to understand each other.

— *Katherine Mansfield*
"The Doll's House"

Choosing a Name

I have got a new-born sister;
I was nigh the first that kissed her.
When the nursing-woman brought her
To papa, his infant daughter,
How papa's dear eyes did glisten!—
She will shortly be to christen;
And papa has made the offer,
I shall have the naming of her.

— Mary Lamb

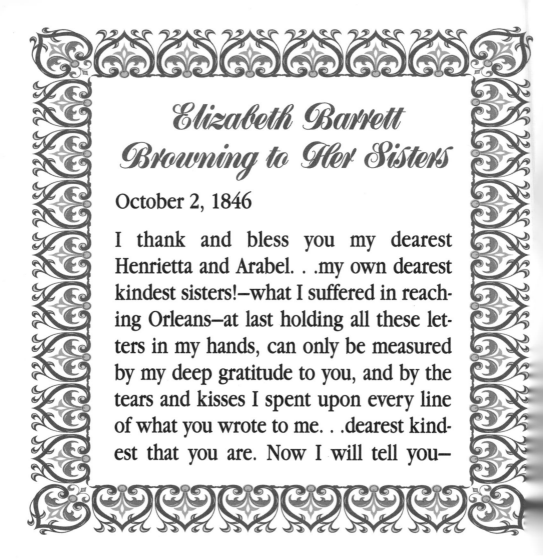

Elizabeth Barrett Browning to Her Sisters

October 2, 1846

I thank and bless you my dearest Henrietta and Arabel. . .my own dearest kindest sisters!—what I suffered in reaching Orleans—at last holding all these letters in my hands, can only be measured by my deep gratitude to you, and by the tears and kisses I spent upon every line of what you wrote to me. . .dearest kindest that you are. Now I will tell you—

Robert who had been waiting at the door, I believe, in great anxiety about me, came in and found me just able to cry from the balm of your tender words– I put your two letters into his hands, and he, when he had read them, said with tears in his eyes–I love your sisters with a deep affection–I am inexpressibly grateful to them. My thoughts cling to you all, and will not leave their hold. Dearest Henrietta and Arabel let me be as ever and for ever

Your fondly attached
Ba

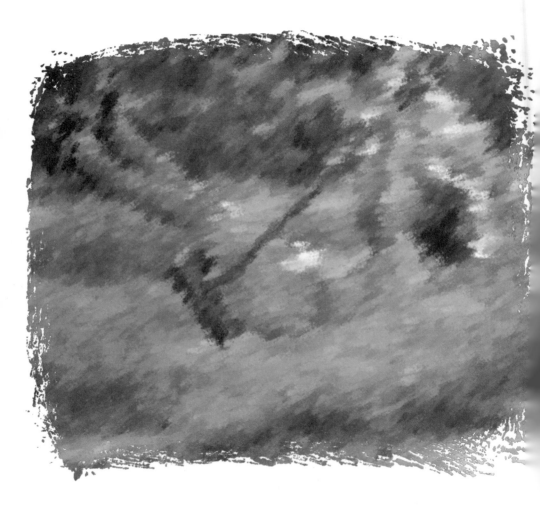

Other things may change us,
but we start and end with the family.

— *Anthony Brandt*

❖ ❖ ❖

There's a special kind of freedom sisters enjoy. Freedom to share innermost thoughts, to ask a favor, to show their true feelings. The freedom to simply be themselves.

— *Anonymous*

During all the years while we were growing up I was fascinated by the contrasts between my sisters. Elizabeth was enthusiastic, loving and devoted. Priscilla was more self-centered and was devastatingly honest about her motives. . .It was Elizabeth. . . whose imagination illuminated–and often transformed in some very special and personal way–the ordinary facts of the workaday world.

— *Margaret Mead*
Blackberry Winter

Sisterly Advice

And if you do see someone with a funny hat, you must not point at it and laugh, and you must not be in too much of a hurry to get through the crowds to the tea table. That's not polite either.

— *Princess Elizabeth, to her sister*

Sisters are our peers, the voice of our times.

— *Elizabeth Fishel*

Celestine and Hortense had been drawn closely together in affection since they had come to live under the same roof, and they formed virtually one household. . . . The two sisters-in-law stayed at home and looked after their children together, and this had created a bond between them. They had come to be so close to each other that they spoke their thoughts aloud. They presented a touching picture of two sisters in harmony, one happy, the other sad. The unhappy sister, beautiful, charged with overflowing vitality, lively, gay, and quick witted, in appearance belied her actual situation; while the sober Celestine, so gentle and calm, as equable as reason itself, habitually reflective and thoughtful, would have made an observer believe that she had some secret sorrow. Perhaps the contrast between them contributed to their warm friendship: each found in the other what she lacked in herself.

Honore de Balzac
Cousin Bette

[My sister] is a bowl of golden water which brims but never overflows.

— *Virginia Woolf*

⬚ ⬚ ⬚

I was always putting myself in my sister's place, adopting her credulousness, and even her memories, I saw, could be made mine.

— *Mavis Gallant*

My sister Sarah is ten minutes younger than I am, making me the older sister, something I lorded over her for years. Until we were about nine, it seemed perfectly logical to me that when I died, Sarah would automatically die ten minutes after me. After convincing her of this obvious truth, we tried to come up with complex plans about how she could be notified immediately upon my death, walkie-talkies perhaps?, and so know that she had exactly ten minutes left. I was very jealous of this: I wanted to be the one to have my life filled with such sudden, however brief, urgency.

— Lucy Grealy
"The Other Half"
Sister To Sister

To My Sister

My sister! (`tis a wish of mine)
Now that our morning meal is done,
Make haste, your morning task resign;
Come forth and feel the sun.

One moment now may give us more
Than years of toiling reason;

Our minds shall drink at every pore.
The spirit of the season.

Then come, my Sister!
Come, I pray,
With speed put on your
woodland dress;
And bring no book; for this one day
We'll give to idleness.

— *William Wordsworth*

My Sister

My sister and my sister's child,
Myself and children three,
Will fill the chaise; so you must ride
On horseback after we.

— *William Cowper*

Where we love is home,
Home that our feet may leave,
but not our hearts.

— *Oliver Wendell Holmes*

$\mathcal{A}$lice was getting very tired of sitting by her sister on the bank, and of having nothing to do: once or twice she peeped into the book her sister was reading, but it had no pictures or conversations in it, "and what is the use of a book," thought Alice, "without pictures or conversations?"

— *Lewis Carroll*
Alice in Wonderland

I'd notice the beautiful faces of my two sisters—their facial bones, their very eyes. Mary was the beauty. She had blond hair and blue eyes and, even as a child, long, long legs.

— *Martha Graham*

Jealousy and love are sisters.

— *Russian Proverb*

Marie Antoinette to Madame Elizabeth

(A farewell to her sister-in-law.)

October 16, 1793

My sister

I am writing to you for the very last time: I have just been condemned to a death that is in no way shameful. . . . I am calm, as one always is when one's conscience is clear. I am deeply saddened to abandon my children: you know that I have lived for them alone, as well as for you, my dear and gentle sister, who through your friendship have given everything to be with me. Where can we find more affection than in the bosom of our families? . . . Farewell, my good and dear sister; may this letter find its way to you! Think always of me; I embrace you with all my heart. . . .

Marie Antoinette

Heirlooms we don't have in our family.
But stories we've got.

— *Rose Chernin*

❖ ❖ ❖

Memory is the diary that we all carry
about with us.

— *Oscar Wilde*

Little Words

"Yes, you did, too!"
"I did not!"
Thus the little quarrel started,
Thus by unkind little words,
Two fond friends were parted.

"I am sorry."
"So am I."
Thus the little quarrel ended,
Thus by loving little words
Two fond hearts were mended.

—*Benjamine Keech*

Sisterly love is, of all sentiments, the most abstract.

— *Ugo Betti*

We have been friends together in sunshine and in shade.

— *Caroline Norton*

My sister Emily loved the moors. Flowers brighter than the rose bloomed in the blackest of the heath for her; out of a sullen hollow in a livid hill-side, her mind could make an Eden. She found in the bleak solitude many and dear delights; and not the least and best-loved was liberty. Liberty was the breath of Emily's nostrils.

— *Charlotte Bronte*

Sisters and friends are God's
life preservers.

— *Anonymous*

The family—that dear octopus
from whose tentacles we never quite
escape, nor, in our inmost hearts,
ever quite wish to.

— *Dodie Smith*

It is a great comfort to have
an artistic sister.
— *Louisa May Alcott*

A sister is a gift of God,
sent from above to make life
worthwhile here below.
— *Anonymous*

Other Penbrooke Books You Will Enjoy:

Love Letters To Remember (ISBN # 1-889116-02-5)
Letters to Mother (ISBN # 1-889116-00-9)
Everlasting Friendship (ISBN # 1-889116-04-1)
Significant Acts of Kindness (ISBN # 1-889116-01-7)
The Little Book of Happies (ISBN # 1-889116-03-3)
A Timeless Gift of Love (ISBN # 1-889116-05-X)
My False Teeth Fit Fine, But I Sure Miss My Mind (ISBN # 1-889116-07-6)

To order additional copies of this book, or any of our other books,
call toll-free 1-888-493-2665

P. O. Box 700566
Tulsa, OK 74170